E♭ ALTO SAXOPHONE   **Book 3**

W9-AJU-982

ACCENT ON ACHIEVEMENT

John
O'Reilly

and

Mark
Williams

The "Keys" to Success: Progressive Technical & Rhythmic Studies in all 12 Major and 12 Minor Keys

Dear Band Student:

Congratulations on completing the first two books of
ACCENT ON ACHIEVEMENT. Book 3 will help you to develop
the musical and technical skills necessary for a lifetime of great
music-making. Your "Keys" to success include scales,
exercises and fun tunes in all 12 major and 12 minor keys.
You'll learn new rhythms and meters, and also improve your
tone and intonation while playing a rich variety of chorales.
With diligent practice, there's no end to what you can accomplish!
We wish you the best in your quest for musical excellence.

John O'Reilly   Mark Williams

Instrument photos (cover and page 1) are courtesy of Yamaha Corporation of America.

ACCENT ON CONCERT B♭ MAJOR

CHORALE: CHILDREN'S PRAYER from "HANSEL AND GRETEL"

Engelbert Humperdinck
(1854–1921)

G MAJOR SCALE (CONCERT B♭)

INTERVAL WORKOUT

SCALE STUDY

CHROMATIC SCALE

ACCENT ON RHYTHM: 9/8 Time

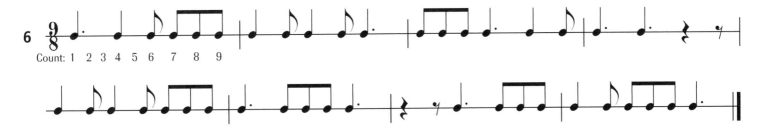

6

Count: 1 2 3 4 5 6 7 8 9

MORNING HAS BROKEN

Irish Folk Song

7

Moderato

mp < mf   mf   mp

ACCENT ON RHYTHM: 12/8 Time

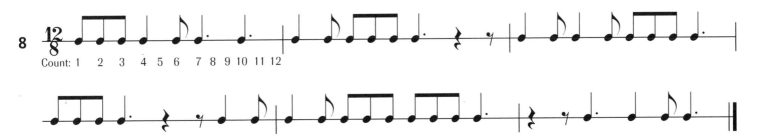

8

Count: 1 2 3 4 5 6 7 8 9 10 11 12

ANDANTE CANTABILE from "SYMPHONY NO. 5"

Peter I. Tchaikovsky
(1840–1893)

9

Andante

mp

ACCENT ON CONCERT G MINOR

CHORALE: BASED ON A THEME BY NEUMARK

Johann Sebastian Bach
(1685–1750)

E MELODIC MINOR SCALE (CONCERT G)

INTERVAL WORKOUT

SCALE STUDY

E HARMONIC MINOR SCALE (CONCERT G)

ACCENT ON RHYTHM: 3/2 Time

15 Count: 1 & 2 & 3 (e) & a

RONDO

Henry Purcell
(1659–1695)

16 Maestoso

Fine

D. C. al Fine

THE WILD HORSEMAN

Robert Schumann
(1810–1856)

17 Allegro

Fine

D. C. al Fine

ACCENT ON CONCERT E♭ MAJOR

CHORALE: BE THOU MY VISION

Traditional Irish Melody

Moderato

C MAJOR SCALE (CONCERT E♭)

INTERVAL WORKOUT

SCALE STUDY

CHROMATIC SCALE

ACCENT ON RHYTHM:

23

THE **K**EEL **R**OW

English/Scottish Folk Song

Allegretto

24

ACCENT ON RHYTHM:

25

PETITE **O**ISEAU

Traditional

Moderato

26

ACCENT ON CONCERT C MINOR

CHORALE: PRELUDE IN C MINOR

Frèdèric Chopin
(1810–1849)

A MELODIC MINOR SCALE (CONCERT C)

INTERVAL WORKOUT

SCALE STUDY

A HARMONIC MINOR SCALE (CONCERT C)

 **ACCENT ON RHYTHM:**

32
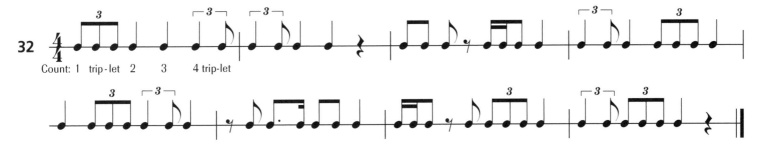

THREE WAYS TO SWING IT

ACCENT ON RHYTHM: *Swing Eighth Notes*

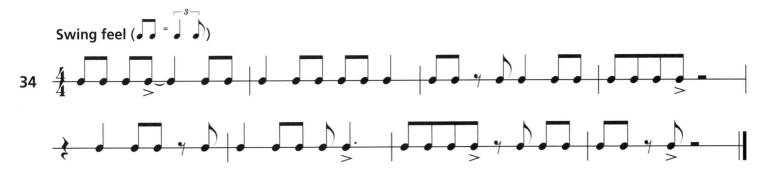

THE BATTLE OF JERICHO

American Spiritual

ACCENT ON CONCERT F MAJOR

CHORALE: SINE NOMINE

Ralph Vaughan Williams
(1872–1958)

Maestoso

36

D MAJOR SCALE (CONCERT F)

37

INTERVAL WORKOUT

38

SCALE STUDY

39

CHROMATIC SCALE

40

ACCENT ON RHYTHM: ♪♫ in 6/8 Time

41

Count: 1 2 & 3 4 & 5 6

THE IRISH WASHERWOMAN

Allegro

Traditional

42

mf

1. 2.

1. 2.

LIP SLUR/FLEXIBILITY STUDY

43

mp

ACCENT ON CONCERT D MINOR

CHORALE: PICARDY

Andante

17th Century French Melody

B MELODIC MINOR SCALE (CONCERT D)

INTERVAL WORKOUT

SCALE STUDY

B HARMONIC MINOR SCALE (CONCERT D)

ACCENT ON RHYTHM: ♪. ♪♪ in 6/8 Time

49

Count: 1 2 & 3 4 5 6

GREENSLEEVES

English Folk Song

Andante

50

mp

mf

mp   *mf*   *mp*

ACCENT ON RHYTHM: ⅞ (Sixteenth Rest)

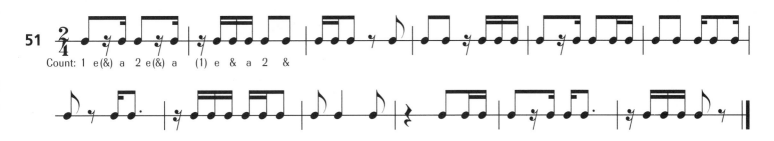

51

Count: 1 e (&) a 2 e (&) a (1) e & a 2 &

LA CUMPARSITA

G. Matos Rodriguez
(1897–1948)

Moderato

52

mf

f

ACCENT ON CONCERT A♭ MAJOR

CHORALE: HOW FIRM A FOUNDATION

Early American Melody

*See Fingering Chart on page 38.

INTERVAL WORKOUT

SCALE STUDY

CHROMATIC SCALE

*See Fingering Chart on page 38.

ACCENT ON RHYTHM: $\frac{5}{4}$ and $\frac{6}{4}$ Time

58

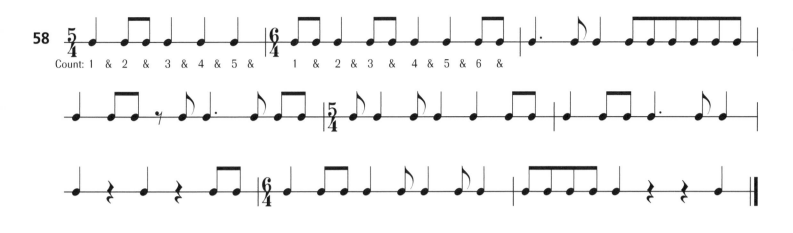

Count: 1 & 2 & 3 & 4 & 5 &   1 & 2 & 3 & 4 & 5 & 6 &

PROMENADE from "PICTURES AT AN EXHIBITION"

Modest Mussorgsky
(1839–1881)

Moderato

59

mf   *f*

mf   *f*   *mf*   *f*

ff

WALTZ from "SYMPHONY NO. 6"

Peter I. Tchaikovsky
(1840–1893)

Allegretto

60

mp   *mf*   *mp*   *mf*

f

mp   *mf*   *mp*   *mf*

mp   *mf*

ACCENT ON CONCERT F MINOR

CHORALE: THE GOD OF ABRAHAM PRAISE

Moderato

Hebrew Folk Song

D MELODIC MINOR SCALE (CONCERT F)

INTERVAL WORKOUT

SCALE STUDY

D HARMONIC MINOR SCALE (CONCERT F)

ACCENT ON RHYTHM:

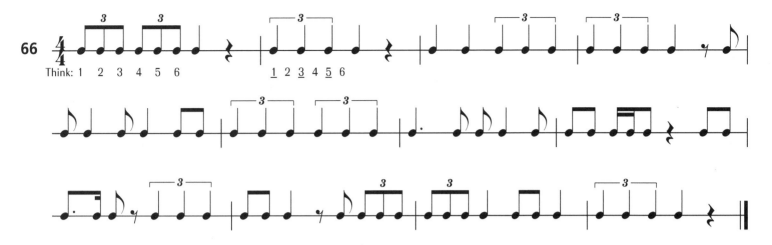

66 Think: 1 2 3 4 5 6   1 2 3 4 5 6

SOMETIMES I FEEL LIKE A MOTHERLESS CHILD

American Spiritual

67 Largo

TRIPLET TUNE

68 Maestoso

ACCENT ON CONCERT C MAJOR

CHORALE: IT IS WELL

Phillip Bliss
(1838–1876)

A MAJOR SCALE (CONCERT C)

INTERVAL WORKOUT

SCALE STUDY

CHROMATIC SCALE

ACCENT ON RHYTHM: *Changing Meters — 2/4 through 6/4*

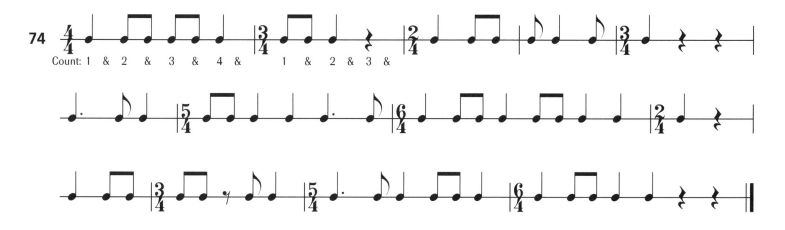

74

Count: 1 & 2 & 3 & 4 &   1 & 2 & 3 &

SOLILOQUY

75 Andante

mp   *mf*   *mp*   *mf*

LIP SLUR/FLEXIBILITY STUDY

76

mf

ACCENT ON CONCERT A MINOR

CHORALE: BASED ON A THEME BY HASSLER

Johann Sebastian Bach
(1685–1750)

F# MELODIC MINOR SCALE (CONCERT A)

INTERVAL WORKOUT

SCALE STUDY

F# HARMONIC MINOR SCALE (CONCERT A)

ACCENT ON RHYTHM:

82 Count: 1 & 2 (e &) a 3 & 4 &

PRELUDE from **"L'A**RLESIENNE**"**

Georges Bizet
(1838–1875)

83 Allegro

CAPRICE **N**o. **24**

Nicolo Paganini
(1782–1840)

84 Allegretto

ACCENT ON CONCERT Db MAJOR

CHORALE: LONDONDERRY AIR

Irish Folk Song

Andante

85

mp

mf

mf   *f*   *mp*   *molto rit.*

Bb MAJOR SCALE (CONCERT Db)

86

*See Fingering Chart on page 38.

INTERVAL WORKOUT

87

SCALE STUDY

88

CHROMATIC SCALE

89

ACCENT ON RHYTHM: Changing Meters — 6/8 and 2/4

90

WASSAIL SONG

Traditional Carol

Allegretto

91

ACCENT ON RHYTHM: Changing Meters — 6/8 and 3/4

92

FIESTA MARIACHI

Allegro

93

ACCENT ON CONCERT B♭ MINOR

CHORALE: KOMM, SÜSSER TOD

Johann Sebastian Bach
(1685–1750)

G MELODIC MINOR SCALE (CONCERT B♭)

INTERVAL WORKOUT

SCALE STUDY

G HARMONIC MINOR SCALE (CONCERT B♭)

ACCENT ON RHYTHM: $\frac{5}{8}$ Time

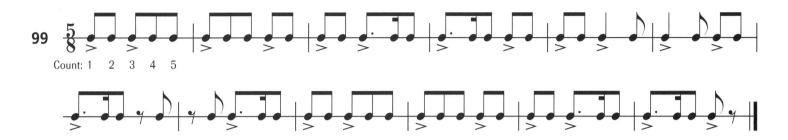

99

Count: 1 2 3 4 5

FUN WITH FIVE

100

Moderato

ACCENT ON RHYTHM: Changing Meters with $\frac{3}{8}$, $\frac{5}{8}$

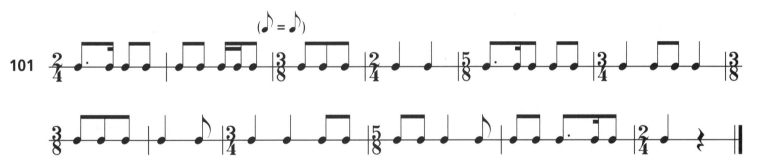

101

VARIATIONS ON A STAR SONG

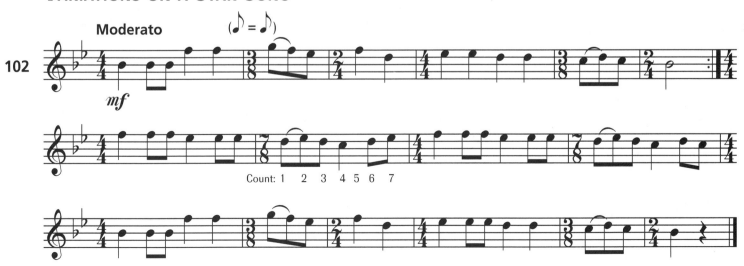

102

Moderato

Count: 1 2 3 4 5 6 7

ACCENT ON CONCERT G MAJOR

E MAJOR SCALE (CONCERT G)

103

INTERVAL WORKOUT

104

CHROMATIC SCALE

105

LA CUCARACHA

Allegretto

Mexican Folk Song

106

AULD LANG SYNE

Andante

Scottish Folk Song

107

ACCENT ON CONCERT E MINOR

C♯ MELODIC MINOR SCALE (CONCERT E)

INTERVAL WORKOUT

C♯ HARMONIC MINOR SCALE (CONCERT E)

LA CINQUANTAINE

J. Gabriel-Marie
(1852–1928)

ACCENT ON CONCERT G♭ MAJOR

E♭ MAJOR SCALE (CONCERT G♭)

112

INTERVAL WORKOUT

113

CHROMATIC SCALE

114

MICHAEL, ROW THE BOAT ASHORE

American Spiritual

Andante

115

mp

MARCH OF THE MEN OF HARLECH

Welsh Folk Song

Moderato

116

f

ACCENT ON CONCERT E♭ MINOR

C MELODIC MINOR SCALE (CONCERT E♭)

117

INTERVAL WORKOUT

118

C HARMONIC MINOR SCALE (CONCERT E♭)

119

THEME from "SWAN LAKE"

Peter I. Tchaikovsky
(1840–1893)

Andante

120

ACCENT ON CONCERT D MAJOR

B MAJOR SCALE (CONCERT D)

INTERVAL WORKOUT

CHROMATIC SCALE

ALLELUIA

17th Century Melody

SHENANDOAH

American Folk Song

Accent on Concert B Minor

G♯ Melodic Minor Scale (Concert B)

126

*Double-sharp: Raises the pitch of a note two half steps. (F double-sharp = G natural)

Interval Workout

127

G♯ Harmonic Minor Scale (Concert B)

128

Hatikvah

Israeli National Anthem

129 Maestoso

ACCENT ON CONCERT A MAJOR

F# MAJOR SCALE (CONCERT A)

130

INTERVAL WORKOUT

131

CHROMATIC SCALE

132

BINGO

American Folk Song

Allegro

133

MY BONNIE LIES OVER THE OCEAN

Moderato

Traditional

134

ACCENT ON CONCERT F♯/G♭ MINOR

E♭ MELODIC MINOR SCALE (CONCERT G♭)

135

INTERVAL WORKOUT

136

E♭ HARMONIC MINOR SCALE (CONCERT G♭)

137

THEME from "SCHEHERAZADE"

Nicolai Rimsky-Korsakov
(1844–1908)

Moderato

138

ACCENT ON CONCERT C♭ MAJOR

A♭ MAJOR SCALE (CONCERT C♭)

INTERVAL WORKOUT

CHROMATIC SCALE

THE BLUEBELLS OF SCOTLAND

Scottish Folk Song

BEAUTIFUL DREAMER

Stephen Foster
(1826–1864)

ACCENT ON CONCERT A♭ MINOR

F MELODIC MINOR SCALE (CONCERT A♭)

INTERVAL WORKOUT

F HARMONIC MINOR SCALE (CONCERT A♭)

HAVA NAGILA

Hebrew Folk Song

Accent on Concert E Major

C# Major Scale (Concert E)

148

Interval Workout

149

Chromatic Scale

150

Home on the Range

American Folk Song

151

ACCENT ON CONCERT C#/Db MINOR

Bb MELODIC MINOR SCALE (CONCERT Db)

152

INTERVAL WORKOUT

153

Bb HARMONIC MINOR SCALE (CONCERT Db)

154

WE THREE KINGS

Traditional Carol

155 Moderato
mp

mf   *mp*

p

mp   *mp*   *rit.*

SAXOPHONE FINGERING CHART

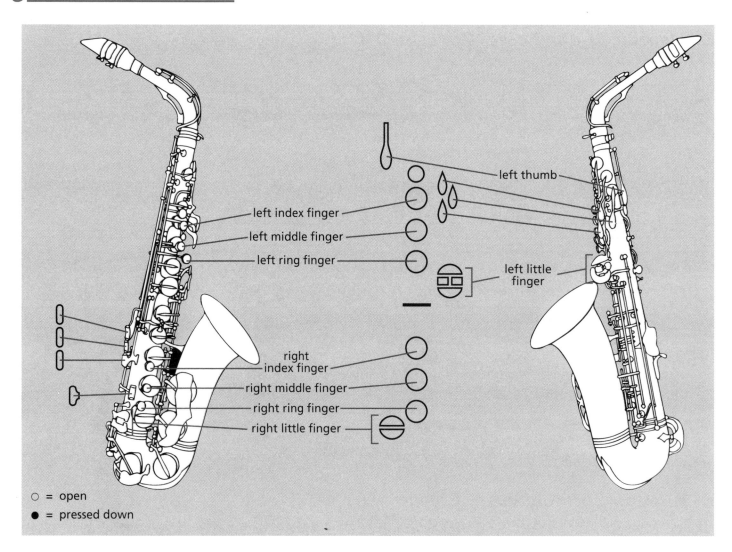

○ = open
● = pressed down

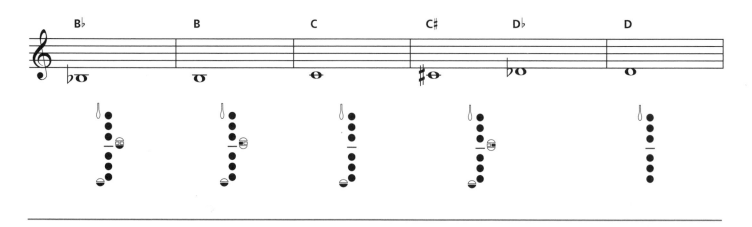

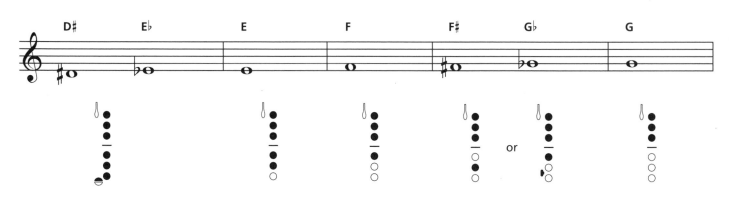

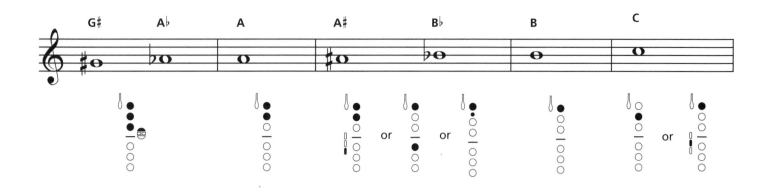

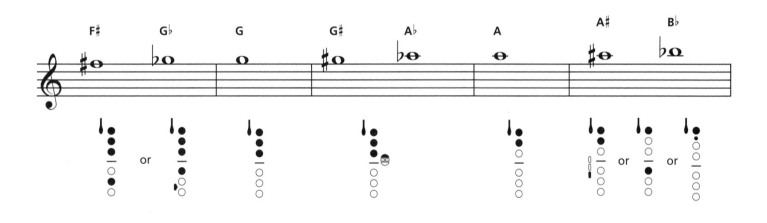

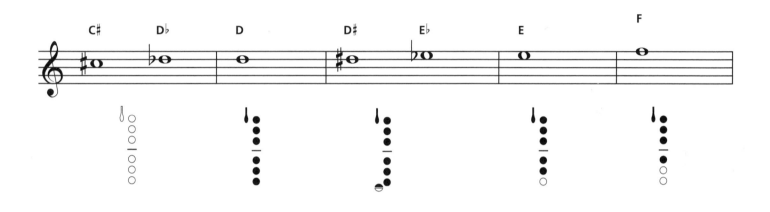

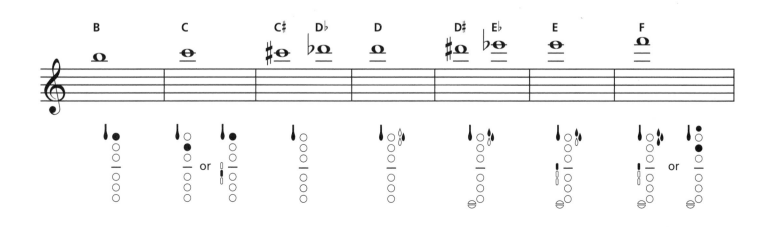

HOME PRACTICE RECORD

Week	Date	ASSIGNMENT	Mon	Tue	Wed	Thur	Fri	Sat	Sun	Total	Parent Signature
1											
2											
3											
4											
5											
6											
7											
8											
9											
10											
11											
12											
13											
14											
15											
16											
17											
18											
19											
20											
21											
22											
23											
24											
25											
26											
27											
28											
29											
30											
31											
32											
33											
34											
35											
36											